TOWN OF SECRETS

Poems by

KATARZYNA BOCZON-DOBBIE

Shoe Music Press

TABLE OF CONTENTS

TO THE OTHER SIDE

The snowbound face of the lake
invites me to wander
my steps faltering
on a slippery surface

I'm going to the other side
of life
to find
what I never had

A moment
held briefly
in the frosty breath of water
allures
promising sparkles in the eyes

My feet learn
the shape of the road
my steps faster and firmer

The friendly womb of the lake
though cold
invites with pleasant light

Looking in the frozen mirror
I can see myself
like I was before
and like I will be

A gentle rustle of the bat's wings
is my guide

I breathe faster
a snow vixen
paints the path in front of my feet

My heart rushing
as I approach the other side

There is a moment
petrified in time and space
of choices unmade
where
the lake of my heart
promises change

I turn around quickly
the rustle of the wings fade
whiteness fills the whole world

I open my eyes
awakened from a deep sleep
betrayed by my own soul

CONVERSATIONS WITH THE MOON

When the silk of darkness
covers the ugliness and infirmity
of the world
I am relieved

Pale light promises
the night peaceful and mysterious
no anger
no hatred
fulfilment of the deepest dreams

I lift my face to the stars
waiting for a cool breath of moon
smiling
he always comes to me at night
if not busy
to listen to what devours my soul
what warms up my heart

Endless conversations
fill up the emptiness of space
the themes crowded at my feet

Night birds listen to our voices
the cry of a fox dies out
when I talk to moon

And then the long walk
fireflies – the drops of night
show us the way

We look in the windows
we look in human souls
stealing into a life not ours

Children's dreams wander in the rooms
lonely people warm up their feet

The busy fall asleep
at unfinished jobs
lovers gift each other
with what you can't buy

And we float
between time and space
nothing hurts
nobody yearns
nobody dreams

I submerge
in the moonlight
falling asleep
to wake up longing
for another night

TIME (THE CLOCKS)

In the world of clocks
there is no past
or future
there is only time
measured equally
by the ruthless arms

Like raindrops
irreversible
the ticking of the clocks

There are clocks for lovers
for those in sorrow and bereavement
for the happy
and for the lost

And each clock
measures different time

Seconds pass
shatter into space
each of them
important only for a moment

The clocks remember
nothing but a particle of an event
jewels floating in space
the events of the clock
are born and die
in the twinkling of an eye

In the world of clocks
silence remains
broken by cruel ticking

Dreams never appear here
lost wanderers
avoid this place

Clocks look at us
with their empty eyes
when we desperately try
to stop the time

Abandoned thoughts
buried
under the tears of all separations
the hearts
that stopped beating for a moment
desires too shy
to be fulfilled

All this accidently
thrown on the burning pile

Big eyes devoid of feeling
look into space
immutably
the world goes on beyond them

ASTONISHED

Awakening from the deepest slumber
I look at you
astonished

It was only
one blink of an eye
and the innocence
quietly tiptoes to the door

Astonished
I touch your faces
they breathe with maturity

Words take different shape
and the voices sound strange
in this moment of anxiety

It's only
a blink of an eye
and you are not mine anymore
and I become an echo
in the chambers of your heart

BREAD

The taste of safety
melting in the mouth
pictures good and warm
line the memory
eyes closed
a moment of non-existence

We will share its goodness
enough loving for everyone
the smell of bread
takes peace
to the heart of the universe

DIAGNOSIS I (INSIDE)

Silence crowded in my head
stone faces
curious
still unresponsive eyes

A box of tissues
smiles with satisfaction
but there will be no tears
though my face is already wet

The universe freezes for a second
an emptiness alone
jostles in my head

I swallow
a silent scream
escape
this word takes my hand
and leads me to the light

DIAGNOSIS II (OUTSIDE)

Voices stayed on the other side
silence with its sticky hand
wipes the sweat off my face
the walls
painfully make wry faces
time slows down
my feet surprised with their weight
try to move with a great effort
I can't see people
their empty eyes
I can't hear silent voices

My mind floats above it all
astonishment overtakes my body
my life shattered into a million particles
in the dark and empty room
of my soul
a tiny sparkle shining
home

DIMENSION IMPOSSIBLE

I can see you peeling apples
I close my eyes
you sit by the window
looking at the immensity
of the night

I close my eyes
and travel through time and space
to meet you
in a different dimension

Quiet...
God will get angry
we are so close
for a moment only

Dimension impossible
a gift from the devil

DOPAMINE

Distrust in my eyes
a little pattern of balls and sticks
that's all
the initials of the goddess of movement
writing scripts of every journey
made by my arms and legs
a substance of life
invisible
rejected by my mind
an emptiness wanders in my head
I look at my clumsy fingers
my feet distrusting
pretend the lightness of movements
expelled from my body forever
dopamine
took away from my blood
all the balls and sticks
slammed the door
not turning round
I fell down for the first time

I MEET SPRING

Wind tangled in her hair
breathless
rushing to the meeting
always late

She brings the fresh breeze
smell of flowers
a beautiful poem

I always wait
she's worth it

I meet spring
in the garden

INSOMNIA

Insomnia dwells inside me
it closes my eyes
when I want to keep them
wide open
it cuddles its creepy face
to my pillow
drinks with me
another cup of coffee
moans in the corners
to keep me awake
it made friends
with all my fears

Insomnia wraps up my heart
with anxiety
it's my sister
my worst enemy
it flows in my veins
like blood
it dwells in my heart
like love

LONELINESS

A dripping tap breaks the silence
waiting
hanging upside down
on the door handle
slow breathing
heartbeat asleep
a sad smile full of hope
an empty plate on the table
a tear
nobody will wipe off...

One-coloured pictures
painted by many brushes
a faded signature
"friends of loneliness"

MOTHER

An absent presence
endlessly wounded forgiveness
wounds once more forgiven
future, past and present
in one single soul united

A life carrying breath
that never falls asleep
pure fulfilment
the essence of love
one heart bathed
in thousands of lakes of tears
mother...

POST BOX

Coolness of friendly metal
shelter of a thousand memories
confessions
rejections
forgiveness and despair

Warm redness
like a great heart
pulsating with a life unknown

Millions of meaningful words
empty lying sounds
wrapped up by soulless paper

Every day you pass
a secret world
unknowingly
submerged in infinite greyness

SCENT OF ANGELS

I turn into my dreams

You take my hand
and lead me to the place
where angels smell
like the evening dewdrops

We merge with the purity of air
transparency flows in us

We are the heart of nothingness
we are the fragrance
of awakened angels

STRANGE ANGELS

Between sky and earth
in the mist of oblivion
strange angels float

With no wings
with no souls
with us they tremble with fear
curl in despair
glow with joy

Strange angels
entwined with helplessness
overwhelmed by fatigue
cuddle into our pillows
in the morning
they don't want to get up
afraid of a new day

Our strange angels
delicate like spider webs
their hearts look for shelter
in the garden of our souls

SWITCH

A switch inside me
writes scripts for my body
on – off
I can – I can't
I will – I won't

A switch decides
when I can write a letter
or take a step

It is my owner
I can't breathe
without its permission

People say
she is lucky
she can just switch off

But they don't know the whole truth

WAITING

The walls stopped moving
breathing heavily
the clocks' arms dropped
the world stopped existing
for a moment
on every lip
silence placed a cold kiss
the heart is rushing
not knowing why
a moment
like an icicle
frozen in waiting

BRIDGE OF SIGHS

I looked for you on the bridge of sighs
dragons' long tongues
were chasing my soul
I touched the ground
where your feet rested
when you were without me
in our places
I kissed the air you breathed
I gathered tears of a thousand separations
which flavoured our moments
I wove a warm blanket made of sighs
and covered with it
searched for shelter from the pain

Bridge of sighs
our place forever
though you are not there anymore
and never will be
the last drops of you
I will gather gently
turn into stardust
and line with it
the path of my heart

CORRIDORS OF MEMORIES

Cold breath of the clock
closes my eyes
I reach out
to touch your face
last heartbeats
it will fall asleep
in the darkness I look for sounds

You are not yourself anymore
like I'm not myself
I squeeze through
the corridors of memories
the remote music
allures with oblivion

I float away
to a land unknown
I will not meet you there
my love dies out
like the cold flame of a candle

I can see a strange face
in the mirror
smiling at me
it's me
the one I wanted to become

The cry of a night bird
steals into my heart
in the corridors of memories
thoughts tangle
I fall asleep

HOUSE ON THE HILL

Lost in time
I keep my dreams in my pocket

I climb over the wall of imagination
to the other side of memory
there is a house hidden in trees
my house on the hill
an oasis of eternity
morning dew paints its walls
silver

I light a fire to warm up my soul
curled under the bed
shivers from cold

I built this house
for this soul of mine
to protect it from the pain and suffering

The house on the hill
abandoned for a while
feels like a stranger now
the empty sound of disappointment
dwells in the corners

LOST SOUL

I gave the Devil my soul

He charmed me with his smile
looked deeply in my eyes
held firmly in dance
and I sold all my poems

In them my soul
entangled inseparably

I wander in the gardens of despair
looking for my soul
shattered into millions of pieces
it flew away
together with my words

An empty shout of a night owl
hurts my loneliness
locked up
in the cage of my own choices
I wash my face
of lies and hatred

An empty space shouts in me
my heart doesn't want to beat
soulless
and I with my soulless tears
paint the memory
of pain and joy

For a beautiful smile
I gave away my poems
to the Devil

PRICELESS SEPARATION

I divorced my insomnia
it left suddenly
without a word
stealing the most beautiful moments

Empty pages
argue on the floor
my pen inactive
nodding off
and the unwritten poems
sing insulting songs
outside the window

The emptiness of disappointments
inside me
and memories
the most precious
of fear
tiredness
and the breath of an owl
that opens its mouth
only at night

Heavy eyelids
tempted with oblivion
first lights at dawn
promise an eternal pleasure

But my soul desires
the one that gave me every night
piercing with fear
a call of an owl

PUPPET IN LOVE

A soft rag heart
beats fast
clumsy hands
look for the way to the face

A puppet soul is filled with warmth
different feeling
unexpected trembling

A puppet love
is an exceptional love
a little body
loves with its whole self
although the strings pull
in the opposite direction
a little heart tightly holds on to love

A wooden figure
curled in surprise
feet look for the way
to the beloved doors

Feet gently caress
beloved footprints

The puppet hands
drip with longing
for the warmth in beloved hands

RAIN DANCES

In the mist
mountains dip their heavy faces
silence
spreads its wings
over an ocean of darkness

Exhausted feet of the dancers
the taste of sweat
raindrops
gently caressing their skin

Rain dances
lift them off the ground
and take them where
the air doesn't know any heat

Their eyes
mesmerised by the rhythm
glow with the excitement
reflecting the tongues of flames

Rain dances
born in the heart of the heat
fed by thirst
plant desire in human souls
rhythmic body movements
entangle imagination
hot skin
like a scorching desert
with pleasure whispers enchantments
as the moment of fulfilment closes in

THE IMPOSSIBLE DREAM

We live at two remote ends
in the land of an impossible dream
I don't know the paths you walk
our hands will never meet

You pass by like a wind
covered with an invisible coat
I can feel your breathing, your smell
volatile
but I can't feel your presence

We are the slaves of the impossible dream
nothing could happen here
the long fingers of eternity
can't reach our souls

I open the window of my heart
inviting a fresh breeze
it brings the promise of unfulfillment
everything's impossible here

Mist covers an empty landscape
I fall asleep with my eyes opened
and turn my face to the cold pillow

TOWN OF SECRETS

In the town of my secrets
the doors don't open
and windows' eyes are half closed
from tiredness

A strange figure is sitting
on the bench in the park
it's me
the same but different

Secrets brush my hair
smiling unwillingly
I absorb their smell
taste their colours

The town of secrets' gates
are closed
no one is allowed to be here
but me

My untold truths
entwine
the lies covered by a veil of sadness

I'm transparent like a stream
comprehensible like an open book
words fill up my soul
secrets fade away in the rain

CHRISTMAS POEM

A taste of Christmas wine
caresses my lips
it's like old times
but without you

The smell of fruit is strong
entwines me
takes me back in time
your hands on mine
when we mixed raisins together

Our Christmas cake
made of our love
togetherness
the story of our lives
forever
always

Winter cold and deep greenness
of the tree
flavoured our kisses
as we made love
in the clouds

The story of our lives
begins with the taste of wine
on your lips
the flavour is still here
the smell hasn't changed

Christmas around the corner
I slip away into my dreams
I open presents
full of memories

Your fingers
drawing stars on her skin

DESERT OF HELPLESSNESS

Hot sand
burns my feet
I close my eyes
fighting the stripping of my soul

Blazing sun
fills the whole world

But
inside me there is still
a memory of a spring
the beginning of existence
purity of thoughts
freedom of feelings

In my mind
I reach out
dipping my fingers
in a cold worship

Non-contamination of mind
renewal
of an unborn child
comes back like a wave

Burning sand
reaches out full of desire
capturing my skin

Here on the desert of helplessness
day doesn't give a rest
swallowing night

There are no directions here
nor good or bad decisions

there is pain
feeding on hesitation
and injections of heat
remind me
how tiny my soul is

FOR A BOY

Nightmares
visited you last night
but I wasn't here
I was away
fighting my own demons

They crawled out from every corner
allured by my insomnia
the grey shadows
spread in front of me
catching my feet

Longing for my presence
you were alone
in the escape
from the depth of monsters' eyes

I wasn't there
when the fire claws
reached for your soul
curling in fear
my absence fed their greed

Nightmares
enchanted me
in the middle of the night
I followed them
not to disturb your beautiful sleep
they set a trap
to keep us apart

I wasn't here
submerged in my own pain
when you looked for shelter
to hide from evil

The tears on the pillow
tell the whole story
I'll wipe them off your heart
with my love

ONE LIFE ONLY

One human life
charmed in a few card boxes
one insignificant existence
on torn pages written
one story of a man
carefully collected for years
blown off by one breath

He was here for a while
he fell in love
and broke someone's heart

He left some crumbs on the table
cold coffee in a cup
and few unfinished poems

It was only a moment
a moment for the universe
a whole life for a man
things collected
priceless souvenirs of life

He built a house
tiny things inside
carefully creating one story

He was here but had to go
asked by gods
and left the puzzle of his life
for others
they pushed it away

In a homeless pile
in front of the house
he used to live

one life buried
one for us only
eternity for him

SHADOWS

Somewhere
in the depth of the night
lost
looking for the way
to the light
shadows of my life
dreams
crystals of my soul
entangled in nothingness

I often visit them
when I close my eyes
they fall
like a silver rain

Sometimes they wipe
the tears off my face
sometimes they gift me
with fear

My life wears a coat
made of shadows
they are always by my side

My angels
My demons

The big book of shadows
opens in front of me
pages smelling
like old age
rustle expectantly

My soul sets off on a journey
the shadows hold its hand

and leads it
to the heart of a dream
there is nothing beyond

SNOW ON THE WINGS OF ANGELS

Melting snow
on the wings of angels
the day smiles at me

I open the window
letting into my heart
the ice cold breath
of your betrayal

It's only a moment
a blinking of an eye
yesterday a heartbeat
today a stone city
of abandoned souls

The wings of angels
covered with stars
though fragile like snowflakes
they will never disappear

In the cave of my memory
poems carved
you carefully put them together
from the rips of your thoughts

There is so much
and so little
in the treasure chest of my love
crumbs invisible for those
who don't have a heart

I cherish dewdrops
like the most precious jewels
I count teardrops slowly
to remember them all

So much pain was born
in one accidental sight
angels close their eyes
removing pain from their faces

UNWANTED

On dream clouds
I sailed to a land unnamed
white-winged doves
showed me the way
a gentle breeze
promised fulfilment

I closed my eyes
absorbed by the journey
in the endless space
a place – an island
of tranquillity and enchantment

I raised my face towards the sun
but all I could see
was a rain of falling figures

But there was no fear inside me

Tiny creatures
children's faces
I floated among them
touching the innocent velvet of their hair
listening
to the music of fragile voices
stories of rejection
and loneliness of their little hearts

They tell about the kindness of angels
their wings as white as snow
that smell like security
there is a place under them
for each unwanted child's soul

I'm back from a long journey

the peace of the story in me
pictures of unwanted existence
charmed in the land of angels

WITCH IN MY DREAMS

A witch
tangled my dreams

At night
she steals in through a keyhole
with a black cat on her shoulder
sits down by the fireplace
and with a crooked comb
brushes her hair

My dreams
intrigued
crawl out of the corners
watching

At dawn
only a piece of my soul
is sleeping by the fire

I trip over
the black cat's hair
tidying up the traces
of last night's madness

Confusion
covers my eyes
I daydream about my dreams
tangled
in the witch's hair

Am I a dream?
Am I real?
Do I dwell only in my own thoughts?
Am I a breath only?

A witch
tangled my mind

YOU AND MY CHRISTMAS EVE

There is a part of me
that can't exist
without you

Though apart
we spend
every Christmas
together

I place you in my heart
cherish you
in my thoughts
when I reach for the presents
I know you do the same

We put the same dishes
on the table
sing the same carols
and over a Christmas candle
we think about those
gone forever

And then you meet the world
covered with a snowflake coat
my heart follows you
keeping you safe
from fear and loneliness
forever

You gave me the taste
of my first Christmas
prepared the path I walk
through these special times
until the feeling vanishes
and my soul fades away

in the breath
of your memories

11TH ANNIVERSARY

I lift up my wet face
covered with tears
tears over everything I lost
over everything I can't have anymore

My heart locked up
my soul swallows the anger
all I can see is my pain
and all I haven't got

Once more
you wait patiently
until I come back

When my legs are tangled
your strong arms
lead me to places I want to see

You don't see changes
and push away ugly pictures

For you
I'm still the same
and I always will be

In your warm eyes
our whole story written
when I touch your face
I can taste that bread in Budapest
when you gently kiss my hand
I can feel the azure breeze
on the Scottish seaside

In your eyes
thousands of memories

disappear
but not forever

I can still find them
every year
when I look in your eyes
to thank you
for all those years

FOX'S TALE

Lonely cry at night
desperately rubs itself
against the bodies of trees
my consciousness wakes up
frozen with fear

When the dark side of my mind
draws the pictures
fainting from pain
another cry of loneliness
tears the coat of blackness

With its tales
it feeds my imagination
the fox of rejection
wanders in my garden

The only one in the universe
the voice of separation
from reality
from the other side of the human soul
from the purity of the world

Terrified with its own cry
the fox cowers
in the corner of my garden

I open my eyes
inviting insomnia
to the room of my existence

I breathe with the same air
as the fox
I taste its fear
feel its longing

My soul once more
follows the fox's tale
I look for the answers
to my questions
of loneliness and fright

IN MY DREAM

You've been here
in my dream
it was only a dream
because
you are not with me anymore

I prepared a meal
and waited by the window
for you
to come back
from your secret wandering

The sky was dark with fear
the wind whispered
disturbing news
but my heart
constant
rhythmically ensured
everything would be alright

My dream –calm
My dream – safe
because you were there
though
you're not with me anymore

I smile gently
at the memory of my dream
I want to go back
to be with you once more

And we will sit
at the table
and you will smile at me
like never before

and for the first time
I'll say
I love you
dad

AUTHOR BIO

Katarzyna Boczon-Dobbie is Polish and writes in both Polish and English. She spent most of her life in Krakow, where in 1995 she graduated from the Jagiellonian University (MA, Oriental Philology; sanskrit). For the past 14 years she has lived in London with her husband, her daughter and son.

Her life took a dramatic change in October 2008 when she was diagnosed with Young Onset Parkinson's Disease.

"My life was snatched from me. For a brief moment I saw all my future plans, dreams and moments of happiness shattered into pieces. I got to know my destiny and that was devastating...But I received something in return. A different way of seeing the world I never had before. Without that terrifying day my poetry would have never come into existence."

She spent the next few months grieving deeply for the person she couldn't be any more; it seemed that life was over for her. In April 2009 she wrote her first poem. It was unexpected for everyone, even herself. Poetry literally became her life-saver.

Since that day she's self-published nine of her own books, created her own website, started Kasia's Poetry Page on Facebook, made over 30 videos and helped others to publish books. In June 2010 she presented her poetry in her home town and in August 2010 her collection of Polish poems was published by Miniatura in Krakow.

www.ingramcontent.com/pod-product-compliance
Lightning Source LLC
Chambersburg PA
CBHW081229020426
42331CB00012B/3099